The Grandmother Book

The Grandmother Book

June Masters Bacher

BAKER BOOK HOUSE
Grand Rapids, Michigan 49506

ISBN: 0-8010-0821-2

Printed in the United States of America

To My Mother
Whose Love I Lean On

About This Grandchild, Lord...

About this grandchild, Lord . . . are You sure I was ready yet? This is no piece of modeling clay You have handed me—a medium that I can shape into my likeness, then place on a shelf for others to admire. In fact, Lord, I'm not sure I can do much shaping. This minute face peeking from a cocoon of pink and blue looks mighty wise to me already. I've patiently tried to explain the schedule around here, but a lopsided smile from this little wizard and I find the schedule won't work any more. I've tried to go about business as usual, but it's hard with warm, fat fingers tying up both my hands. Are You sure, Lord, You sent the baby to the right house? I mean I wasn't even a very good mother—at least, I don't think I was. I kept fumbling and stumbling. Will I be any wiser now?

About this grandchild, Lord . . . are you sure my credentials are in order? I've had no experience, you know. What is a grandmother supposed to look like? Act like? *Feel*? Right now, other grandparents assure me, all I have to do is diaper and feed this newborn child. *Sustain*, they call it. But isn't sustaining more by Your definition, Lord? This particular baby is different—flesh of my flesh, blood of my blood—with a whole built-in set of characteristics no other baby ever had. Am I up to helping the child develop the talents You gave and backing off when I'm not needed? You see, in all the hustle-bustle of preparing for this third generation, nobody checked on my qualifications. Are my legs ready for circus time and wandering around at the zoo? Am I ready for "choo-choo train" play and no's when they are needed? I've forgotten about princes in golden towers . . . and I'm not even sure I remember what to do about bee stings and croup.

Somehow, today I'm seeing the world from a whole new vantage point. I know I ought to be dusting while the little one sleeps—and I've no idea what tonight's dinner will be. But, instead of taking care of these matters, I keep looking out at butterflies on the wing. Were they always this lovely, Lord? Yes, I guess they were . . . I remember those in my grandmother's petunia bed . . . somewhere I have a picture. I find myself wanting to look through the family album to see just which of us this tiny bundle of humanity looks like . . . I am remembering the pictures my parents took of me . . . and those I took of my son. Already this baby has formed a new link between my grandparents, my parents, my child, and me. I feel a peculiar sense of continuity that wasn't there before. I stand in awe and wonder at this cradle I've put to use for the third time down through the years and feel that—well, You'd given me a third chance at life, Lord. I feel myself growing a new personality—or rather an enlargement of the old—as I begin to grasp what has happened to me. You've created for me a new tomorrow.

About this grandchild, Lord . . . it's pretty grand—it really is—to be a grandmother! Just lend me a hand now and then. I'll shape up the second time around.

Grandmother's Rights

By virtue of bloodline, you have attained some rights and privileges that accrue only to those who are similarly situated. There is now a new heir to the throne, your grandchild.

You have acquired the right to be a target for jokes and to take some ribbing at times—because of all your experience, your willingness, and your eagerness to pass it on! You have also been granted the privilege of having your cooking—particularly chocolate-chip cookies and gingerbread boys—held up as the epitome of epicurean delight in later years.

To you has been granted license to wonder if your son and your daughter are adequately prepared to mix formula with good sense. You have become qualified as a judge to pass upon the manner in which another household besides your own is organized and run to adequately and sanitarily take care of another guest. It is your duty to see that law and order are maintained, while seeing to it that there be no corporal punishment!

In addition to all this, upon you has been bestowed something you have not had before: another relative, whom you will love, honor, cherish (and, possibly, at times obey!) because the parents had the good sense to give the child your name (if not the first name, surely the last—if neither, to know that your name will be mentioned with affection).

And, to you has been given the crown for as long as you shall reign—the precious crown of *grandmother*—which you will wear in pride for as long as you both shall live.

My Grandmother's People Plants

It was always fun to help my grandmother bring the family's favorite houseplants inside for the winter. Both of us complained a lot about what a bother it was, but the plants knew we were enjoying ourselves. They could tell by our singing. Holidays were just around the chimney corner, so we sang little Thanksgiving hymns and Christmas carols. Our potted plants must have felt a stir of anticipation, because they added new leaves and bloomed out of season.

Nobody else could understand why our plants stayed awake to enjoy the holidays instead of dozing off for the winter. Yes, we oiled the leaves with castor oil and picked off the occasional dry leaves, my grandmother told them. And I explained how much the plants enjoyed their sunny window by day and the night-long warmth of the fireplace. But neither of us told that we sang to them and read them stories. The two of us had unlocked a secret of the heart—only we had no idea, of course.

"These flowers thrive on all the attention they get," my grandfather said grudgingly. But there was a certain pride in his voice—especially after I brought home from school the information that green plants released oxygen

in great big gobs, replacing what the fireplace inhaled. And the plants went right on growing and blooming to brighten the winter chill. We had our reward. . . .

Plants are catching on these days. Florists' pots are a lot more decorative than our red clay ones used to be. There are superspecial minerals and vitamins and there are books and books of personal histories for every domestic plant. There's something called an aquameter to measure the water level. There are articles galore about light and shade preferences of plants, how to dust them, and how much fluid their systems require to throw off a virus. The one my mother and I smile about is the suggestion that one should catalogue the musical preferences of plants. Titles would help, but composers are even more in keeping with growth: Beethoven, Bach, boogie-woogie, or a bit of the brogue will inspire them to do their morning calisthenics. "All this will make them grow," experts insist. I hope so. This world needs a lot of blossoms and the air these days needs all the oxygen it can handle. So the plant thing is great—no greater, of course, than when Grandma and I coddled ours against the East Texas cold. And none of the writers say a word about *love*. . . .

It was sort of fun, really, having those plants ready to separate and repot for gifts, or being able to pluck an out-of-season bud and take it to a shut-in. Grandma used to say the gifts did people more good than the pills they swallowed. Maybe she was right, for her patients seemed to bloom like her plants. "There is always a pressing need for friendship," she said. True. And people "grow better" with added attention, too. Grandma was right in saying, "They blossom and bloom in the rich environment of love—and the reward potential is far greater."

So now, even though I live in a warm climate where plants thrive happily through the four seasons out-of-doors, I remind myself frequently that it is time to bring *people* to the indoors of my heart—the way my grandmother did. It takes so little to make others happy, actually—a word, a smile, an understanding glance. The air becomes more bracing with loving response. That's the secret Grandma and I discovered together so many years ago.

Small Things, Remembered

Recollections are tricky. They tend to enlarge to impossible circumferences — due largely, I guess, to the countless handspans our memories add to small things. Looking back, it seems to me that I always knew I lived in a world of magic that other people are very late in discovering and labeling antique.

My world was lovely to live in. I remember brocade drapes drawn against the summer sun to keep the parlor carpet from fading. The carpet was a garden of cabbage roses with a crisscross path worn through the middle where two generations had greeted each other as they hurried to bedrooms, dining room, kitchen, upstairs, outdoors, or into one of the mysterious rooms that "stored things" in the long ell.

It's the "stored things" I remember with greatest clarity. Each treasure took on a personality all its own because of a person or an incident connected with it. Maybe I recall only fragments. I can never be sure. However, it seems that each little incident happened over and over as if determined to stamp itself in my memory. If I could convince myself that I have never had a dream, and awakened only to drift into the same dream again and again, maybe I would shed my conviction that I attach numerous recollections to each fascinating item in the mysterious dark of the ell of childhood.

At first there were only big pieces stored in the spare room. They waited for the family to come for them. The extra brass bedstead was for unexpected guests, those who spilled from the guest room, were unable to find sleeping quarters with somebody three-to-a-bed, and did not mind the hall or living-room traffic. My mother says the tornado only touched down once, but I am convinced the same storm swooped down like a hungry hawk every night that memorable March — and every March thereafter.

I remember watching in terrified fascination as ice-white claws of lightning dug at a mulberry sky. Thunder that might well have heralded the end of the world . . . swirls of dust . . . the sound of breaking glass drowned out by deafening rain . . . and then the awful roar. My grandmother's wash was on the line. I watched it turn inside out and then lift up and soar through the late afternoon like magic carpets . . . and then there *were* carpets . . . rooftops . . . and the dead silence that was louder than the terrible roar.

What gets us through those things? Then, it was neighbors. We seemed to be the only ones left with anything to share. And suddenly it all seemed very wonderful! Beds and cots went up like Arab tents and tomorrow, just as suddenly, I knew they would be gone. I determined to make the most of it. "I will sacrifice my little bed," I said like a six-year-old angel — then happily squeezed myself onto the brass bed where six other children were sleeping crosswise. . . .

There was an extra potbellied stove in the ell — a stove somebody said Benjamin himself once owned. The year of the awful freeze (they tell me it only happened once,

too!), we brought the little stove into the bedrooms, one by one, to warm the corners the back-to-back fireplaces wouldn't reach. "I'll warm you a brick for your feet," Mama said. To this day, no electric blanket can replace that remembered warmth. . . .

There was a treadle sewing machine that had belonged to my great-grandmother. It was solid oak with fancy cast-iron legs and treadle, a combination that made it so heavy two men had to carry it into the parlor when Mama wanted to mend. She would allow me to open the flaps, but the head of the monster was too heavy for me to lift. Sometimes when my mother had thrown the sewing machine out of gear for safety's sake, I could fill the bobbin—pumping away for dear life with both feet on the treadle. Oh, the magic things that machine could do on command! I'll never forget the fairy dresses—I *know* there were lots of them, all blue—that I wore for the Maypole dance. I was "Faith" and my mother said that's what it would take for her to finish the dress on time. I didn't worry, for if she failed to finish that spring, there would always be another and I would always be "Faith."

Mama pressed the blue net of the eternal dress with a set of flatirons she kept hidden away until Tuesdays, when she ironed. When one of my uncles gave me an entire set of Harold Bell Wright's books, my mother wanted to display them and used the flatirons for book ends. We should have copyrighted the idea. We'd have gotten rich, I am sure, judging by the number of people who thought of displaying their collector's items in the same manner. We were the first, of course!

There was a clock stored there—a clock which had lost track of time. Never anywhere have I heard of an invention like it. It, too, was oak, with a set of Westminster chimes. Once it sat upon our mantle, but it lost its place because of its strange behavior. It chimed faithfully on the quarter-hour, but it struck on the quarter-hour, too. By the time it had made a complete cycle, it had struck four times. Daddy said it was "dishonest." I doubt if he wanted to get up at three o'clock when the alarm on the Big Ben was set for six. Once Mama tried to bake a cake by it. The guests never reappeared. Neither did the clock. They all departed the same day. . . .

But it's the little things that I remember most. Just why the family had saved such things puzzles me. The magic of it is that they did save them. On rainy days I used to go into the dark room and drag one of the several boxes to the window. We used coal-oil lamps, but my

mother wouldn't allow me to take a lamp into the room alone — and alone was the only way I could go back into the wonderful memories that people told me only happened once and relive them the many times I knew they happened.

There was, for instance, a coil of clothesline left over from when Daddy stretched the line from post-to-post of the fence, above the barbed wire. Then, one time when we aired my grandfather's red underwear, the bull charged the fence. It *must* have happened a hundred times. No animal could gore a garment that many times in a single battle. Oh, it was funny . . . I would rock with laughter, except in the presence of Gramp. That's another reason I liked solitude.

There was a wire popcorn popper — the kind you hold over an open fire. The bottom was burned out of this one because the night the preacher came I suggested we treat him. Brother Boggs insisted on holding the contraption. It caught fire. Mama screamed. Daddy ran for water. Grandfather saved the day, but lost out with Brother Boggs. The fire had loosened the paint on the handle Gramp grabbed. "Aye, Gunnies!" he screamed . . . and I rolled in merriment till my ribs ached, but the minister thought the language was "as dangerous as the fire."

There was a "Faultless" starch box with a collection of "Faultless Stories" tucked inside. How I loved those! They came with every box, telling that the boiled stiffener was so powerful it could do this and that, and the illustrations proved it. They showed ladies stiffened at the broom, boys riding bikes with their legs straight out, things like that. I used to watch the expressionless face of "Ole Aunt Jo," who sometimes helped with the wash, and feel sure that she, too, had sampled "Faultless." It would have been better, though, if I hadn't told her. My grandmother overheard. . . .

Tenderly, I would put all the treasures away when Mama called. I'm glad I knew their worth even then. Somehow I always knew that, although they happened over and over (I know they did!), some day they would stop.

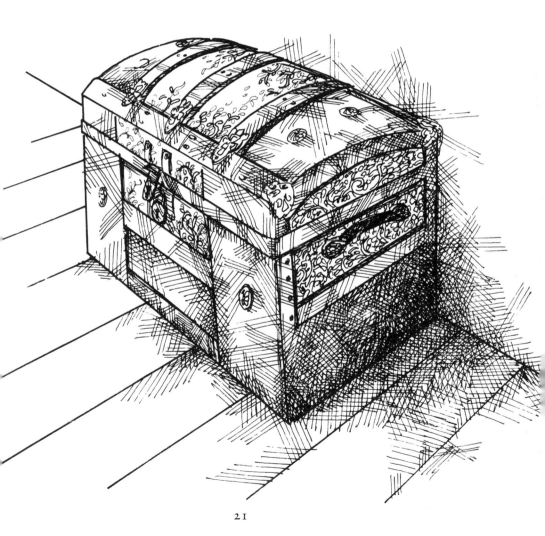

Grandmother's Valentine

Back in the garden-days of youth
When February came,
You chose a rose and sent to me
With card that bore no name.
What matters now the colors gone
From cheek and bloom once fair,
Or timely sifts of silver on
My once near-raven hair?
I've kept the roses in my heart;
I know I always will—
And as the special day draws near,
I feel the same sweet thrill . . .
So let my silver crown descend;
Sweet memory makes it shine;
My heart recalls each daily rose
From you, my valentine.

New Wisdom

Pink roses wrap the old rail fence;
Wild berries stain the hill;
Each thrush has learned a song of love —
Their throats are never still.
Someone, one day, more wise than I
Will tell me how a spring
Lets flowers know it's time to bloom
And tells the birds to sing.

But until then I like to think
That earth-things know somehow
That their response can make my heart
More wise than it is now.

Give Us the Spirit of Easter, Lord

Give us the spirit of Easter, Lord, which is *believing* — believing in others; believing in ourselves; and believing in our capacities to grow, because of love You gave.

Give us the spirit of Easter, Lord, which is *renewal* — renewal of our faith in You, our strength, and our "spiritual fitness."

Give us the spirit of Easter, Lord, which is *gratitude* — gratitude for Your unquestionable goodness; gratitude for our loved ones; gratitude for the arms of springtime which surround us with April's glory; and gratitude for Life beyond life — the message of this season.

Give us the spirit of Easter, Lord, which is *joy*! Let us laugh. Let us sing. Let us enter this season with such a heartful of joy that never again can those around us speak of Easter as a historical event. Let us make it the living message You intended — the same yesterday, today, and all the tomorrows to come. Let us sing it. Let us shout it. Let us reflect You in our joy.

Give us the spirit of Easter, Lord, which is *love* — perfect love, not such as we are able to give but such as the love which You gave us and we, through You, are able to reflect.

Give us the spirit of Easter, Lord, which is *knowing* — knowing that Your love never fails; knowing that the sun continues to shine behind each April cloud. Let us know that love is eternal even when, momentarily, we are unable to experience it. Let us know without doubt that You stand near when we fail to feel Your presence.

Make our hearts glad with *hope*, Lord. Make us hear the promise of this blessed season and find *peace* within our hearts. *Give us love and more love, Lord, which is, indeed, the spirit of Easter!*

A Basket of Love

For, lo, the winter is past, the rain is over and gone; the flowers appear on the earth; the time of the singing of birds is come, and the voice of the turtle is heard in our land. [Song of Sol. 2:11–12]

Our entire Western world is ready to burst into bloom or song. We watch for a robin, a crocus, a shift in the wind. We need a sign, we say, to reassure us that the white world of winter is turning green. We long for songbirds, laughter of thawing streams, and the smell of growing things. We are winter-weary.

But what about the winter-weary hearts around us — those who will know no springtime unless the rest of us care? They, too, need signs.

This Easter I'm going to weave a basket — a basket so big it will hold 365 gifts! Those gifts will cost nothing, but they will outlast daffodils, pussywillow, and colored eggs. They will come in assorted shapes and sizes, a something for everybody I meet each day. And my basket will be filled to overflowing when another Easter comes, because no matter how much it shares, my basket will hold love and more love — like Easter!

1. I'll give everyone a smile;
2. the broken-hearted, a shoulder to cry on;
3. the person who tries (even though that person fails), a pat on the back;
4. a loved one a hug or a kiss (for no reason);
5. a stranger, a warm handshake.
6. I'll sing even when I'm down (who knows how many will hear my song and pass it along?);
7. try to laugh when the joke's on me;
8. consider the other person's point of view;
9. ask for forgiveness when I'm wrong;
10. forgive others when they wrong me (even when they fail to ask).
11. I'll write a letter to a friend who owes me a letter;
12. offer to help a new neighbor unpack;
13. write a "thank you" to a manufacturer of pet food my dog will eat;
14. thank the newsboy;
15. ignore the new spots on the carpet;
16. praise someone I admire (and envy just a little).

I'll feed a stray cat . . . play frisbee with the children next door . . . give to the poor anonymously . . . pray for those who don't ask me . . . and say "I love you" every opportunity I have. . . .

My list will grow longer and longer — like the lengthening hours of daylight. Warm days will come, and the little buds — like hearts — will open. And almost before I know it, the world will have turned green from the tidal wave of love. Every bough, stem, and branch will blossom. Those who needed a sign will have seen one. "Someone cares," they will say. Winter will have fled. And my basket will overflow.

Small Deeds Recalled

Sometimes when you're tired
And the road is rough,
All hope holds its breath
And you've suffered enough,
Just sit down and count
The friends you have known:
And you'll find yourself
No longer alone.
Beside you there'll walk
A memory dear
Of someone who spoke
When you needed cheer . . .
Another who made
Some sacrifice small:
A second mile walked . . .
A telephone call . . .
A warm, friendly hand
That helped you along . . .
Another who sang
A bar of some song . . .
Refreshed, you'll push on
And manage to smile:
Such small deeds recalled
Make this life worthwhile.

Returning to Dream

I dream of a fire
From a hickory log;
A tortoiseshell cat,
An ever-wet dog
That hover around
Its welcoming flame—
How often I wish
Things stayed just the same. . . .
I dream of a rocking chair
With a broad lap . . .
The velvet-soft purring . . .
The singing of sap;
And an old kettle
That joins them in song:
I marvel that memories
Linger so long.
The house is deserted;
The hearthside is bare;
But I'm glad that loved ones
Left doors open there.

Food for Thought

I'm a mixture of cook and teacher.
"But which do you teach?" ask they.
"I teach small children," I tell them—
"To measure their work and their play."
"Will you share that recipe with us?"
"I'm no formula person," I say.
"Each takes a special blending,
And ingredients change some each day:
One child needs sorting and sifting;
Another a gentle pat;
But all need a dash of affection.
They simply won't rise without that!"
So, with courage and sometimes misgiving,
I roll up my sleeves and begin
That special gourmet assignment
Of molding gingerbread boys into men.

We Ride Back on Small Things

A memory can visit
In some surprising way:
There comes a sound of reapers . . .
A scent of new-cut hay . . .
A blush of ripened purple
From hiding berry patch
That creeps along the creekbank
And stores find hard to match . . .
A sudden field of larkspur,
Soft lavender and blues . . .
Company come to dinner . . .
The feel of Sunday shoes.
Bright calico of quilt scraps . . .
A cozy featherbed . . .
The scent of honeysuckle
Mixed in with baking bread . . .
A path one loves to follow
That cuts across the woods . . .
The peddler with his backpack
Of other-worldly goods . . .
The schoolbell ringing sharply
Through summer's-ended air . . .
The sadness when you're going,
The gladness when you're there . . .
And then the paired initials
Upon some ancient tree
Printed in a heart-shape
And signed *To you from me.*
So let the world keep turning
And wipe our tracks away,
Let us ride back on small things
And visit yesterday.

Cradle Quilt

The quilt that cradled as sweetly you slept —
Did you trace its pattern of memories kept?
Captured in abstract
Circle and square
To cross-stitch distance
From Here to There:
A block of black velvet
From Granny's chair;
a first-day-of-school skirt,
Locks of your hair;
An ivory petticoat's clinging caress,
A taffeta whisper of wedding dress —
Cloth-binding of a patchwork of shapeless things
Created from chaos and given wings.

This Old Lot

This old lot's a sort of landmark
Where in springtime and in fall
All the young ones used to gather
For a game of childhood ball
While their parents looked on proudly
Till the sun was sinking low,
While the parents of their parents
Talked of "days of long ago. . . ."
Now the weeds have taken over—
No outfielders tramp them down—
Yet the old charm seems to linger
On this lot in my hometown.
I can almost hear the voices,
Visiting of this and that,
Till their own son (or a grandson)
Proudly went to take the bat.
Then the shouting and the screaming
(As if winning meant a crown!)
Till the loved one reached "home" safely—
In this lot in my hometown.

Each Age
a New Adventure

Each age brings with it an entirely new set of adventures, opportunities, and challenges. It is well to remember that the previous stage has not ended; rather, it has blended into the new one to enrich and to beautify.

Remember how, as a child, you used to run with the wind to your back until your young heart hammered against your ribs? Remember the smell of damp, raw earth after the first spring shower? The beauty of the first crocus? The feel of Mother's understanding arms when you'd run your hardest and still lost the race? Remember the thrill of getting the lead in the school play? Passing an exam in math that you were sure you failed? The triumph of your first soufflé? Your step was buoyant. Your heart was light. Each sunrise was painted with expectancy.

And then you "put away childish things," for you were growing up. You gave a slumber party . . . joined a club . . . and met a someone so special that the mention of his name made it unnecessary to use the rouge you were experimenting with. Oh, life was lovely, lovely. . . .

Then came the adventure of going away to school, followed by the excitement of your first job. Remember

the thrill of a first paycheck? None of it compared, of course, to meeting your mate — the vows made and kept — and the choosing of a few installment-plan pieces of furniture to go along with the wedding gifts and Grandmother's four-poster bed made more beautiful by Mother's hand-pieced quilts. The years slipped away somehow and suddenly, it seemed, the house overflowed with the laughter of the children. . . .

And now you learn that you are to be a grandmother. A new adventure! A new set of opportunities and challenges. And, yet, there are some misgivings. "The years have taken their toll," you say. "The thought of a fresh start frightens me a little. It is a different world today —."

True! But you have changed, too. You have the wisdom that only experience can bring. Recently, a group of apprehensive grandmothers-to-be came up with this list of suggestions.

1. Take each day a step at a time.
2. Focus on the baby-to-be, not yourself.
3. Stop putting yourself down; you reared one of the parents, didn't you?
4. Stop offering flimsy excuses and learn to do something well, or review what you think you have forgotten.
5. Learn to analyze your shyness. All things considered, aren't you just as capable, interesting, and creative as the grandmothers you see around you?
6. Above all else pray:

> Lord, this is the beginning
> Of a new age—a new adventure—
> One that You have entrusted me with
> To use as I will;
> I can worry it away
> Or I can use it as You have ordained.
> Teach me to draw upon my yesterdays
> And lean upon Your arm today
> So that when tomorrow comes
> I will have traded a segment of my life
> For something wonderful—
> The leading of tiny footsteps
> Into Your Kingdom.

This stage, too, will pass. And one day you will look back with pride—knowing that nobody else could have done quite as well!

Stitch by Careful Stitch

... you ... [are] a partaker of the glory that shall be revealed. [I Peter 5:1]

Stitch by careful stitch my grandmother used to work at her embroidery. As a child I watched her patience as she punched the needle in and out in an effort to follow the almost indistinct pattern she had traced by means of a piece of worn carbon paper.

"What will it be, Grandma?" I would ask.

"You'll see by and by," she'd promise.

And, sure enough, eventually the pattern suddenly bloomed into a tulip, a rose, a baby elephant, or a line of Dutch children wearing wooden shoes. How beautiful it was—a lovely gift for each of us.

There are days in our lives when we, too, must work stitch by careful stitch. Days that take patience. Days when the pattern is almost indistinct.

It is good to know that, like my grandmother's embroidery, the pattern is there. And we must make it bloom.

Each of us has a pattern. God traced it in our hearts from His perfect design. It is up to us to make that pattern into a "tulip" or a "rose"—something beautiful that blooms according to His plan.

Let me take this day a stitch at a time, Lord, as I work patiently on the pattern for my life so that when I have finished, I will have left something beautiful for my children—and my children's children. Amen.

Grandma Always Told Me...

bits gleaned from the 50 states

"It is a rare man who can forgive the person he has wronged."

"Rudeness is a little person's imitation of importance."

"The person who gets ahead is the one who does a little more than is necessary — and keeps on doing it."

"Hold your anger, but a little righteous indignation can work wonders."

"It's so easy to criticize — so much better to get in and help."

"You must learn to do things when they ought to be done."

"Always wear clean undergarments . . . what if you were in a wreck?"

"A person is about as big as the things which make him angry."

"It always snows once more after the robins come."

"It takes a good driver to be careful."

"It is easy to tell the other fellow why he should be patient."

"Always do a little bit more than is required."

"The best way to forget your own problems is to help someone else solve one."

"It is always easier to command than to convince."

"Measure twice and cut once."

"It takes a lot of luck to make up for a lack of common sense."

"Nothing is as hard to do gracefully as getting down off your high horse."

"It is always easier to hate something than to understand it."

> If a task is once begun,
> Never leave it till it's done;
> Be thy labor great or small,
> Do it well, or not at all.
>
> Here's a bit of wisdom
> That's found on China's wall:
> "A big man never thinks he's big;
> A small man, never small."

Kitchen Tales

Some fifty years ago or more she made rag rugs for
   this rough floor
To warm her children's baby feet while baking bread
   for them to eat.
She churned and hummed a merry tune and canned the
   fruit of early June
To save and serve on winter days — preserving things
   were Granny's ways.
She scrubbed young faces, braided hair, planned
   "Sunday clothes" for them to wear;
And as she washed and mended clothes, she told the
   stories Mama knows.
Now I have children of my own, but memories I've
   not outgrown;
My entire household's richly blest with kitchen talks
   I've saved for "best."

Children

Children are God's apostles, sent forth day by day, to preach of love, hope, and peace.

James Russell Lowell

I have often thought what a melancholy world this would be without children; and what an inhuman world, without the aged.

Samuel Taylor Coleridge

God sends children for another purpose than merely to keep up the race. They are to enlarge our hearts; to make us unselfish and full of kindly sympathies and affections; to give our souls higher aims; to call out all faculties to extended enterprise and exertion; and to bring round our firesides bright faces, happy smiles, and loving, tender hearts.

Mary Howitt

Blessed be the hand that prepares a pleasure for a child, for there is no saying when and where it may bloom forth.

Douglas Jerrold

The smallest children are nearest to God, as the smallest planets are nearest the sun.

Jean Paul Fredrich

Lord, give to men who are old and rougher
The things that little children suffer,
And let keep bright and undefiled
The younger years of the little child.

John Masefield

And Jesus said of children, ". . . of such is the kingdom of heaven." [Matt. 19:14]

Unwrapped Gifts

Such precious gifts, unwrapped, unsealed,
Come every day from you:
No sentiments, no bows or strings—
Just little things you do.
Just yesterday your little hands
Came knocking at my door;
You handed me a daffodil
And then went back for more.
All day my heart leaped up with joy
Because the tiny bloom
Was more than just a daffodil
That you brought to my room.

To Pray Is...

To remember Grandma
And her ready knee
With Bible spread wide open
So little eyes could see. . . .
And to go out walking
Before the dew was gone,
Recalling what she told me —
That I was not alone
As I watched for bluebirds
And softly touched each rose,
Or looked for rainbow-bubbles
In tubs of dirty clothes. . . .
Then to catch a bunny
And warm it with my hands
And contemplate in silence,
Then say, "God understands."

I Believe in Grandmothers

I believe in grandmothers—
Tall ones, short ones,
Chubby and thin,
With big patch pockets
For hiding things in.
I believe in grandmothers—
Older ones, younger ones,
And in-between
Who say we're successful
When towels are clean!
I believe in grandmothers—
Who give us the moon
And show us a star
By letting us know
We
    outshine
        them
            by
                far!

Grandmother's Legacy

Grandmother dear, you could not give
A royal crown to me
But taught me how to make leaf hats
Beneath my sweet gum tree.
You could not offer purple robes
With ermine for a trim
But taught me to wear simple capes
And to walk tall in them.
Some people boast of royal blood—
To this you made no claim;
And yet you taught me to take pride
And guard the family name.
You could not send me voyaging
To some far-distant shore
But sought a woodsy path instead
Where we could both explore.
We could not hear operas
In some great concert hall;
But you sang old, familiar hymns—
You must have known them all.
You'd never read great books, you said,
You never had the time;
And yet you knew each Bible verse
And every nursery rhyme.
You did not know psychology,
But you dispelled each fear:
"You never are alone," you said,
"For God is standing near."
You showed me busy ants at work;
New lambkins out at play;
"Your heart is where your treasure is,
So store," you said, "then play."
You owned no gold; earned little fame;
And knew no royal birth—
Yet through your humble teachings I
Inherited the earth.

Lavender Dreams

The scent of lavender always brings
The country-sweet smell of growing things:
Lilac buds pouting after the rain;
Hand-painted china . . . some old refrain . . .
Fresh-laundered linen, packed in a chest . . .
Last rays of sunset left in the west;
Trails of bur clover . . . bloom of the sage . . .
Ribbons on letters, yellow with age . . .
Hint of a sunrise tinting the snow . . .
Long-looked-for letter . . . something called *hope*;
Wallpaper roses; Grandmother's soap . . .
Nothing is stronger than color, it seems,
Wrapping my world in lavender dreams.

Good Friends
and the Seasons

What is friendship? Is it not the warmth and beauty that comes when we possess a wide circle of close friends whose constancy we can count on? Like the seasons, friends return to us year after year—in spirit, flesh, deeds, dreams, and memories—each time bringing a new sense of wonder, discovery, and delight. . . .

Spring is the handshake of a new friend. A shaft of exploring sun touches the dominant browns of winter with brightness. The trees, though bare, look less faded in the new light. A frog calls from the pond, hopefully awaiting a reply. A rested beaver surfaces and experimentally stretches its full length in the unexpected warmth.

Skunk cabbage, down in the hollow, grow bold. Tired of their last year's shapeless shells, they shamelessly shed them in exchange for rich, new foliage. Hickory trees dangle catkins like a headful of emerald curls. The woodland, so recently somber gray, opens one eye while the other dozes. Soon, so soon, if the visiting sun returns, the countryside—like a giant canvas—will come alive with a rosy blush. Already the maples on the hillside, eager to make a good impression, hastily form pale pink seed—shaped for flight. Reeds, astonished at their own growth, send up new shoots ... green upon green stretches across the drabness of the marsh. The world takes a deep breath of April air. *It is the time of sowing.*

Summer is the tightening clasp of a growing friendship. March winds relax. April fills earth's cup with rain. One feels the balm of approaching summer. Living things bask in the "perfect days" of the season. Meadow flowers reach from clod to sky, congregate, and clump along the fence rows. Raucous jays debate loudly beneath a high-noon sun, then settle conversationally in the willows as if their differences were settled. Ducks rest on the maple-shaded pond and the beaver goes on with his dam. Peaches are plump and ready for canning. Bare feet make trails in the morning dew — welcoming its cool. Weeds surrender to the gardener's hand; but, tenaciously, the crabgrass remains ... the season is beauty and sweet-ness — leaning on the arm of care. Neglected, it will go ragged and wild. *It is the time of growing and nurturing.*

Autumn is the affectionate arm around the shoulder of a friend. August stops sulking at the first September rain. A sort of gentleness sets in as summer yields to fall. A mysterious haze changes the perspective of the land-scape. Hills are more distant, more aloof; trees are closer together as if in thought; and the atmosphere is spiced with quince. Farmers fill silos with fat pumpkins and peanut-hay. Bright-eyed field mice search the stubble for overlooked grain. Ducks on the pond muffle their voices. An indefinable sense of satisfaction mellows the world with a shawl of loveliness.

A crisp north wind lifts the luminous haze, reveals the

fire that the aspen and pin oak have kindled on the hill-sides, and mingles the odors of wood smoke and maple syrup. The sunshine has more substance, as if it were melted down. October's bright, blue weather is a fleeting interlude to be loved, cherished, and remembered when stronger, sharper winds have stripped the trees of color and the birds have flown away. The foot of anticipation steps toward Thanksgiving; the foot of reluctance holds back . . . but the theme of autumn is harvest. *It is the time of storing.*

Winter is sitting down with a seasoned friend — talking and remembering. . . . Fat bears have gone to sleep. Wasps have abandoned their gray-sponge nests and given up their sting. Night becomes a quiet thing. The glow of the moon deepens; the flirtatious stars wink through November's thickening clouds — lighting the way to eternity. A first snowflake . . . a shimmer of silver on the pond . . . the cry of a lost goose in need of company . . . a beaver reaching for one last twig — and nature beds down for the long, white sleep.

December's world adds another back log and reaches out for family, friends, and neighbors to insulate against the cold. Now there is time for togetherness as families tramp the woods for holiday greens, as neighborhoods plan meetings and parties over the choicest fruits they have planted, nourished, and harvested in the preceding seasons. The wise gardener took proper steps at the right time to insure that efforts would not go in vain. Winter is now the glad day of rest . . . an angel smiling in the snow . . . all the beauty and sweetness of spring, summer, and autumn unfolding in life's reality: Love! *Winter is the time of sharing.*

What, then, are the seasons? Are they not the warmth and beauty that come when four seasons of our lives —

all different — accept the common Cause in God's world? Like loving friends, the seasons return to us year after year, with a constancy we can count on — in wide and wonderful range to show us the rewards of learning the goodness in those who are unlike ourselves when love is greater by far than opinions, beliefs, and habits, and binds us with the golden thread of understanding.

Family Ties

If God has taught us all truth in teaching us to love, then He has given us an interpretation of our whole duty to our households. We are not born as the partridge in the wood or the ostrich of the desert to be scattered everywhere. We are grouped together, brooded by love, and reared day by day in the first of churches, the family.

Henry Ward Beecher

The family was ordained of God that children might be trained up for Himself.

W. Aikman

A happy family is but an earlier heaven.

John Bowring

My Heart Is Content to Remember

My heart is content to remember
The treasures of life's little things;
The thrill of a child when it's snowing;
The trill of a robin in spring. . . .
My heart is content to remember
The worth of each gem in the dews . . .
The circus is here and we're going . . .
The pride in a new pair of shoes!
My heart is content to remember
Fulfillment a grandchild can bring;
It fills to the brim, overflowing
With pleasure in life's "little things"!

Finding God

I find God in the lilies
So pure, so clean, so bright;
I find Him in the sunrise
And in the folds of night.
I find God in the silence
When I kneel down to pray;
And in the "Hallelujahs"
I hear on Easter day.
I find God in my gladness
And mingled with my tears,
In first cry of a baby
And in the stoop of years.
I find God in the prayer-wings
That soar to realms above —
And, yet, I never met Him
Until I learned to love.

. . . for God is love. [I John 4:8]

Hand-me-downs

I used to hear the kettle sing
As if it heard the prayer
That Grandma said to start the day
While rocking in her chair:

"Lord, you have given me this day
And planned the tasks for me;
Just simple things that hands can do
To serve a family.
I thank you for these kitchen walls
And window with a view
Where I can watch loved ones come home
When their day's work is through.
Teach me nobility that lies
In loaves of fresh-baked bread
So my heart finds fulfillment when
My family must be fed;
And let me know when my day ends
That I have done my best
With tender crust and loving heart—
Then, I'll have earned my rest."

The years have rocked away somehow
(I guess they always do);
I wonder if you knew, Grandma,
What I would learn from you?
I hear the ancient kettle sing
As if repeating prayer
That Grandma handed down to me—
From her rocking chair.

A Child's Dilemma

I hate those pants my gram'ma makes and leaves me
   room to grow;
They make me look all jittery because they wobble so!
Why do the pockets on the side slip clear 'round to my
   seat?
How come the trousers wrap my legs and tie up both
   my feet?
One day I turned the pants around — I didn't think
   she'd mind;
But that just complicated things — the zipper went
   behind!
I've got to tell my gram'ma 'bout how hard it is to go
With pants on hind-before at school — 'cause she left
   room to grow!

I Wish
to Thank You

I wish to thank you for the joy
You've brought to me each day;
For smiles which hold an inner glow
When I have lost my way.
I thank you for the patterns set
In all you say and do;
All the trials you have met
And how you've seen them through.
I thank you for your gracious deeds —
More than you'll ever know —
Without grandmothers, pray tell me,
How would we children grow?

Grandma-love

Some day I hope — I truly do —
I'll be a grandma just like you
With asters growing in a row
Where butterflies and fairies grow . . .
And there'll be trees for hide-and-seek
And cookies baked fresh every week.
I'll try out every recipe
For gingerbread and potpourri
Made from roses wet with dew —
When I some day am "Grandma," too.

Some day I hope — I truly do —
I'll be a grandma just like you
Who calls the beetles all by name,
Tells every story, knows each game,
Who smiles and hums a happy song
With every child who comes along . . .
I'll mend each dolly just like new
Then hug its owner as you do —
And maybe then the world will see
What Grandma-love has done for me.

She Shall Be Praised

Who can find a virtuous woman? for her price is far above rubies.

Strength and honour are her clothing; and she shall rejoice in time to come.

She openeth her mouth with wisdom; and in her tongue is the law of kindness.

She looketh well to the ways of her household, and eateth not the bread of idleness.

Her children arise up, and call her blessed; her husband also, and he praiseth her.

Many daughters have done virtuously, but thou excellest them all.

Favour is deceitful, and beauty is vain; but a woman that feareth the LORD, she shall be praised.

Give her the fruit of her hands; and let her own works praise her in the gates. [Prov. 31:10, 25–31]

I Know a Place

I know a place that character built,
A place where great sacrifice
Was made to bring joy to all others;
I called it my paradise.
I know a place where happiness dwelt,
Where true love took its abode
And offered wide arms of shelter
To feet grown weary of roads.
Square feet would not measure the distance
From front door to the back;
Its spirit lit eyes of the children—
Windows that brightened night's black.
A sign said, "Come in without knocking,
Strangers no longer need roam,"
Its atmosphere whispered a welcome—
My memory of Grandmother's home.

Memories of Broken Bread

The loaves of bread Grandmother made
Were never fortified
With supplements of this and that
And yet they satisfied.
The feather-light and yeasty loaves,
Oh, golden-good the smell!
As if to nourish us with love
And hunger quell as well.
Sweet memory of cooling loaves —
A still life of delight —
Preservatives? Preposterous!
Loaves would not last the night!
And so it was we broke our bread —
Those brown and tender crusts
That reached to heights unknown today
Sustained by love and trust.

Here and There

Happiness is first a choice. Later it becomes a habit.

There is a bridge that leads to heaven. Each little act of kindness you do makes it more secure for others who pass this way in search of life's other side.

Sociologists say a child's play is his work. A grandmother says it is the job of the parent to turn a child's work into play.

"Without the people a vision perishes," I once heard a grandmother say. "Without vision the people perish," the university sign reads — which is the proper quote. But I am glad nobody corrected the great lady.

Children, like flowers, are untroubled by calendars and almanacs. When they feel warmth after a gentle rain they just come popping out to take a look at the sun.

June Masters Bacher

My Window Helps Remember

This window place was special
Where the kittens curled
And my happy children
First viewed the outside world.
'Twas here I did my mending—
Minding not at all
As I watched green springtime
Turn to amber fall.
'Twas here I saw my garden
I've planted one for years—
And though the need is gone now,
I shed no foolish tears.
Though families may scatter
We're never far apart
When windows help remember
By framing in the heart.

A Household Hint: "Let It Stand!"

Great-grandmother's *Household Hints* is more of a treasure than any of the new cookbooks in my library today. The writing is quaint and the sentence structure would spell despair for grammarians.

Some of the recipes are great. I have tried them. Others call for ingredients I have never heard of and so I am forever asking my mother's generation. I am fortunate enough to have known my great-grandmother and her daughter, my grandmother, but I was too young then to care about what went into their magic dishes. Mama can help me somewhat, but she and I agree that it would take Solomon to unriddle some of the recipes.

The most mystifying and intriguing are listed under "Handy Household Hints." Here are a few of them. See how many of the ingredients you recognize and the methods you understand.

The hand-sewn book containing the recipes of my great-grandmother and her neighbors is falling apart, but I cannot bring myself to have it rebound, any more than I can correct her English. Most of her concoctions end

74

with "Let it stand . . ." so I think I shall just follow her directions.

Soot stains: Soot falling from open chimney can be swept up without a heap of trouble by sprinking lavishly with salt at first then sweeping.

To clean kid glove: A good-sized piece of light-colored flannel, some laundry soap and sweet milk. Put glove on, put flannel over finger, moisten by merely dipping in milk, then rub on cake of soap and apply to glove. Rub toward ends of fingers, changing flannel as it becomes soiled, being careful not to get the flannel too wet or let gloves dry on hands.

Cleaning fluid: One gallon deodorized benzine, one ounce chloroform, one ounce ether, two ounces alcohol, one ounce oil of cologne. Do not breathe.

Varnish and paint: Use turpentine on coarse goods; on fine goods, alcohol. Sponge with chloroform if a dark ring is left by turpentine. Stay away from fire.

To wash easy: Put over the boiler with one-half or two-thirds full of water. Cut up two tablespoonfuls of paraffin and one-half bar of lye soap and melt in a quart of water. Let boil up and add this to the water in the boiler. Wet the clothes, wring out and soap dirty places. Put in and let boil twenty minutes, stirring once in a great while. Take out and rub on a rub-board, rinse in seven waters and hang on line or barbwire fence to dry.

To clean wool: To five cents worth of soap bark add one and a half pints of water. Boil half an hour and strain. Brush goods and spread smooth. Apply warm liquid with flannel cloth to right side, pressing on wrong side until dry. Will make old look new unless it felts.

For cleaning bathtubs: Wipe with moistened cloth with kerosene. It will disappear completely.

For cleaning silver: Take a pound of whiting and pour

one quart of boiling water, stand aside until cold, then add one tablespoon turpentine and ammonia. Shake and stand away until wanted.

Furniture polish: Half pint benzine, four ounces Golden Japan, three ounces linseed oil, three ounces carbon oil. Rub on hard.

Tar: Soften the stains with hog lard, then soak in turpentine. Scrape off carefully with a knife and rub gently until dry — no matter how long it takes.

Soot stains: Rub spots with dry cornmeal before sending them to the wash pot.

Mildew: Soak in a weak solution of chloride of lime for hours; rinse if the water is cold. If it stays there, wet the cloth and rub on soap and chalk mixed together, and lay in the sun; or try buttermilk or lemon and lay in the sun.

Grass stains: Rub molasses on the spots, then wash the garment to remove the molasses.

Wooden bathtubs: If they go to stave, instead of filling them with water which sure will go stagnant, just paint them with glycerine. The wood will not shrink until the glycerine dries and that may not happen for months. If it does, just do it again.

Good soap: Good soap for those who do rough work like tending fires and sifting ashes is made by melting good soap and stirring in Indian meal until it is thick, then adding one teaspoonfull of tincture of benzoin.

To exterminate moths: An ounce of gum camphor, one shell of red pepper, macerated in eight ounces of strong alcohol and strained. Sprinkle furs and wrap them in sheets.

Most any recipe works better if allowed to stand till mellowed.

Shortcuts to Happiness

I used to like green-apple pie. I doubt that I would any more. It was puckery even then. But youth is impatient. Who on earth would wait for apples to ripen? Stomachaches wouldn't have kept me from the forbidden fruit, but one look from my parents did. A green-apple pie was a compromise. Two hours of waiting outstripped two months.

I used to like double-feature movies. What's more, I sat through them twice. Now, I can't sit through the minutes of the last PTA meeting without yawning. But, at thirteen, from one Saturday to the next adds up to more than a week. It's a lifetime. I would have wasted away had I not found a creative way to shorten the work week. Eight hours in the local movie house got me through forty in the classroom. A ratio of one to five seemed fair . . . if only I could reverse the setting.

I used to like collecting tinfoil — particularly gum and Eskimo Pie wrappers. Rolled into a ball, the foil sparkled and glowed and set my salivary glands into overtime. I named the silver wad my Good Luck Ball and endowed it with magical powers. "It will bring you luck before the sun sets," I promised each gullible friend who touched it. What *kind* of luck depended on whether they contributed a wrapper to its growing circumference — and gave *me* the gum or ice-cream bar. Cavities in baby teeth were of no consequence in those days. Waiting *was*. Only Fridays were chewing-gum days if I lucked out. That's when I took eggs to the store for Mama. The odd pennies were mine to spend. But the change came out even more times than I like to remember!

I used to like picking up insulators along the railroad tracks. Would I stoop to that again? Well, maybe — were the glass as jade-lovely now as then. How beautiful the insulators were — row upon row of miniature emerald castles, straight from the Land of Oz. I lined every wall but was forever in search of more. That meant that I must tag along behind the boys who dared violate the mores of our community. They boldly ignored the warning sign: Ladies and Gentlemen Will Not — Others *Must Not* — Break These Insulators. I watched with envy their

"good chucking arms" bring down a few without breaking them. Then there was no criminal offense, was there?
"You may pick up only the insulators which fall," my
mother said. Like leaves — once a year? Like stars — once
a light-year, or whatever calendar they used to fall by?
"Yes, Mama," I promised. All insulators fell, I knew,
their falling frequency in direct proportion to accuracy
of aim.

I used to like being chased by the boys. The chasing
game began in first grade. Come to think of it, it's the
only childhood game that the years seem unable to change
. . . then it was wrong, not illegal-wrong or undesirable-
wrong, but *verboten*-wrong. I was never able to make
my parents or teachers understand why we girls *had* to
be chased. Only those who couldn't learn the alphabet
or wore long underwear were left out. My mother came
down with something she called a "vexing headache."
My teacher expressed "distress at the underlying cause."
My grandmother, on the other hand, possessed more
insight than was good. "Leave 'em be. Last week the
hound pup was chasing the colt. This week it's the colt
chasing the pup. They about ruined my garden with their
chasing — till this morning when they met face-to-face.
Dog gave a woof, colt gave a snort, and both hightailed
it." Oh, dear, I wouldn't want that to happen. Still, waiting to grow up took a long time — maybe more time than
I had. I slowed down a bit as time wore on.

I used to like rising yeast dough . . . divinity before it
had "set" . . . jaw-locking taffy before it was pulled . . .
my bangs irregularly chopped with the kitchen shears
before haircutting time . . . stockings rolled down to ex-
pose my knees before the spring thaw . . . carrying my

buckle-on boots while wading across the creek to take a shortcut . . . *shortcut*, that's it! A shortcut to happiness.

Well, what's wrong with that? I've outgrown the blue dress I wore to my first party, but I still love the color. Apple pie and insulators, tinfoil and movies have lost a certain charm. But from them and the other likes that only children seem to understand, I've sorted out some lasting values. Why waste a moment? Why wait? Everything has its season: the heavy sweetness of petunias in bloom, sun on rain-damp earth, the sad whine of a fishing line, snowballs, and kites. I light candles at breakfast instead of waiting until dinner. I eat my birthday cake before it is frosted. I do not bank on Fridays or use the freeways on weekends. And each day I chase a little dream — but avoid a head-on collision.

All that's fun does not have to be waited for. Memories are valuable property — molded in childhood, but not restricted to children that we were then. Memories are — well, *shortcuts*, shortcuts of the mature eye which focuses on subtleties of what we have become.

Here's to a happy today!

Recipes and Family Trees

I'm holding Great-grandmother's book,
From which she taught Grandma to cook—
Who shaped, in turn, the dough for tarts
To demonstrate fine kitchen arts
For my own mother, then for me—
A book can be a family tree!
And so it is my firm belief
That I must add another leaf
For generations after me—
To whom, one day, "Great-gran" I'll be!

Cobweb Dreams

There's an organ in the parlor,
Stilled by time its silent keys;
And the empty room is haunted
With its echoed melodies.
I can hear them in the evenings —
Mellow notes like chimes they rang —
I can feel the aching sweetness
Of the old songs that they sang.
Youthful feet knew just which pedals —
Pumping sweet, familiar song
Into corners of forever,
That hearts, leaving, took along.
Eager hands turned fast the pages
Of sheet-music memory,
Sending notes where none could find them —
Drifting to the "used to be."
But it's here I sense a presence
As close now as then, it seems —
Gram's still seated at the organ,
Anchored by time's cobweb dreams.

Notes from Home

A house is built of logs and stone,
Of tiles and posts and piers;
A home is built of loving deeds
That stand a thousand years.

Victor Hugo

Look well to the hearthstone; therein all hope for America lies.

Calvin Coolidge

You can no more measure a home by inches, or weigh it by ounces than you can set up the boundaries of a summer breeze or calculate the fragrance of a rose. Home is the love which is in it.

Edward Whiting

We need not power or splendor;
Wide hall or lordly dome;
The good, the true, the tender,
These form the wealth of home.

J. S. Hale

When home is ruled according to God's word, angels might be asked to stay with us, and they would not find themselves out of their element.

C. H. Spurgeon

Every house where love abides
And friendship is a guest
Is surely home — and home, sweet home —
For there the heart can rest.

Henry Van Dyke

Painted Dreams

Who can paint a dewdrop
Fading on the lawn?
Who can paint a sunset
When the sun is gone?
Who can catch on canvas
Dust from shooting stars?
Who can paint a birdnote;
Line and space the bars?
Who can paint a zephyr
Playing in the trees?
The young and old together
Can see and store all these.
Children see the vision
Through older eyes, it seems,
So future generations
Can share love's painted dreams.

And it shall come to pass afterward, that I will pour
out my spirit . . . and your old men shall dream dreams,
your young men shall see visions. . . . [Joel 2:28]

Especially for You!

An Anniversary Wish
for Grandmother
from Grandfather

You are very special
In every dreamed-of way;
And I feel sentimental
On this, our special day.
I think of all our laughter,
Sprinkled with our tears—
But would I have things differ,
Could I relive those years?
No, each one is a love-gift,
Wrapped up in memory—
So thank you for each moment,
This anniversary!

Song
of Autumn Time

Dear Lord in heaven o'er us,
For earth-joy, sky, and seas,
Sliced sunshine in the meadows,
And shuffling feet of trees
As russet leaves surround them —
  We offer thanks for these.
We thank you for the springtime,
The whispered-rumor breeze
Which promised earth a rainbow
When ice-thaw heard its pleas
And gently watered orchards,
Then roared out to the seas;
For summer and sweet clover,
Green garden herbs to please,
Fevered brow and parching throat,
Refreshing winds that tease
Eagles into backward flight —
  We offer thanks for these.
Soon winter will enfold us
And still the hum of bees,
And Someone tells the fur-folk
Of after-harvest ease;
Ponds pull their shawls around them
Against the misty breeze;
Fat pumpkins squat in hiding
Under corn tepees.
How comforting the fireside,
How blest the eye that sees
The blessings of our country —
  We offer thanks for these.

Silhouettes of the Past

As a grandmother, you are undisputedly the family historian. You've shown the family album, answered a million questions, and perhaps made a family tree. You are now in a fine position to suggest that the grandchildren do some recording for future generations to find. Here is an activity that is guaranteed to turn any ordinary day into a memory-maker. Maybe you will want to plan a special time; or you can take advantage of any day one or several of the youngsters come to visit.

"We are going to record the past in much the same manner that ancient peoples communicated with their neighbors," you can begin by saying. And the real attention-getter comes when you promise your grandchildren that the activity will be a little like cave-writing! "Only you will use a rolling pin instead of a writing pen to make clay tablets for future generations to find."

When it comes to finding a pattern, it's hard to beat the fine hand of nature. Take a leaf, for example. Each is different in color, shape, and design of the veins. Each can tell its story in pictures when pressed into clay.

Make an adventure of looking for leaves — each child selecting a favorite leaf. The color doesn't matter; but the larger the veins are, the better they will show when molded. Press the leaf flat between the pages of a magazine and leave it overnight (if time allows). At least, leave it pressed while, together, you make the clay.

Mix together one and one half cups of cold water, one

cup of cornstarch, and two cups of baking soda. Place the mixture in a pan. Stir over a low heat until it is about as thick as synthetic clay. Let the mixture stand until it is cool enough to handle. Then place the warm clay in a foil pan and cover it with a damp cloth until it cools.

Knead it into a ball and place it into an airtight container until you are ready to use it. Many foods come from the market with plastic lids ready to be placed on top once the cans have been opened. These make good storage containers.

Meantime, the leaf has flattened out and is ready to take its place in history. Pinch off a small ball of clay and lay it on a hard, cloth-covered surface. Roll smooth with a rolling pin. (And remember that *your* grandmother taught you a smooth bottle would work if you have no rolling pin.) Make each tablet about one-fourth inch thick and two or three inches wide (or, if you are working with a very large leaf, enlarge the size of the clay so that it is a little larger than the pattern). Hold the stem with one hand while rolling the leaf so there will be no risk of the leaf's slipping and creating a double image. Working in pairs helps.

To finish the silhouette, lift the leaf and place the clay tablet bearing its imprint in a 250-degree (Fahrenheit) oven for several hours to "cure" it. After the tablet cools, each child can paint the leaf silhouettes with pastel shades of water or tempera paint, touching the outline lightly with a small brush. The remainder of the slab should remain unpainted. After the design is dry, a coat of clear nail polish or shellac will protect the finish and add a glossy look.

The child's name and the year should go on back of the plaque. Use a pencil for this purpose; or plan ahead and print the information on the back with a nail while the clay is still damp. Just another record of a happy day!

Tell ye your children of it, and let your children tell their children, and their children another generation. [Joel 1:3]

A Sort
of Touchless Touching

My grandmother told a bleak story that fall, and all her dire predictions came to pass. A bad winter we did not need in 1934. We were in the grip of the Great Depression — certainly no time for Old Man Winter to clench his fists. "But there's no reasoning with the seasons," Gram'ma declared. "I reckon they've no ears — just voices." By "voices" she meant signs, a favorite topic for my maternal grandmother and her folklore-weather-prognosticator friends.

All signs pointed to a harsh winter, the six ladies agreed, on that autumn afternoon which should have been beautiful but wasn't. Usually, by October, the lowering sun sent shafts of light through thinning, colored boughs of sweet gum, oak, and dogwood, reminding me of stained-glass windows with candles burning behind them. I recall one of my childhood poems began, "October is a month of flame. . . ." I had the golden glow of the colored leaves in mind, of course. The only flame that year was the relentless sun which burned the countryside to an ugly brown and heated each breeze that passed.

It would be difficult for one unsteeped in such matters

to accept "the signs," I suppose, but I had grown up with them, so it would have been equally difficult for me to discredit the predictions as my grandmother and her friends quoted adages, nodded in agreement, and rocked and fanned themselves on an afternoon just out of the oven.

I was always fascinated with Miss Fannie Mae's accounts — not that she was as well informed as Gram'ma, nobody was — but Miss Fannie Mae received frequent reports from kinfolk back in Wisconsin. They had bears there. So what if there were none of the furry creatures in East Texas? The signs were for all places. Nature just used different animals for mouthpieces in different parts, and it was the job of human beings to share the "knowings."

Gram'ma took over. "Squirrels are hoarding nuts and chattering like they're telling us to prepare. I'm right glad the acorns didn't fail like the gardens. All the hoarding's a sure sign of a tough winter all right."

Granny Carson spoke up, "Things don't augur well with the woolly worms this year. The furry crawlers got the blackest coats ever this year — sure-fire way to foretell a bad spell. They're hurrying across the slab, too!" Granny knew about railroader signs. Her husband was a retired train conductor.

My grandmother nodded. "Really black. 'The lighter the coat, the milder the winter,' " she ended with a quote.

It was Granny Carson's sister, who was visiting from Alabama, who shed some light on the "tree-dwellin' grasshoppers," and, of course, it was Gram'ma who set her straight with a word, "katydids."

"Whatever — they been hollerin' since Fourth of July," the Southern lady volunteered. "Leastwise, down there."

"Well, that means a killing frost by October fourth. You can figure a hundred days from the time they start."

The facial expression of my grandmother portended disaster.

After the company left, I begged my grandmother to share more signs with me—not that begging was necessary. "Remember the fog back in August? Never saw the likes of it." That was true. Fog was very rare in our area, but I had never thought of its being a bad omen.

"And the wasps' nests. The critters generally choose my lilac bush. This year they built right down on the ground. And the woolly mullein down on the branch; why, it's head-high."

Mullein usually grew to be knee-high to me, and my nine-year-old knees were near enough to the ground to measure a low-growing plant. The mullein was a good seven feet tall that year. But why? "Got nothing to do with the growing season. It just knows to get up extra tall before a severe winter so the birds and mice can feed on top of the snow. Snow's going to be higher than your head. I guarantee it."

I whistled in anticipation. The whistle brought Esau. "Looky! Now, I ask you, did ever you see so thick a coat on a canine? Why, the dog looks like he's ready for shearing."

Esau did look more grizzly than usual. He appeared to have no eyes at all, but he made his way to the old oak tree in the back yard. "Notice the bark?"

I wasn't sure if my grandmother was speaking of the sheepdog or the tree. "Thick layer on the north side's building up for a raw winter." It was the tree, then.

The raw winter came—worse than Gram'ma had predicted, worse than I could have imagined, worse than even the old-timers had witnessed in that part of the world. I shudder recalling it. What little canned fruit we had — very little, since nothing matured that year and we had to depend on wild blackberries along the branch — froze in the jars. I remember the ghostly sight of frozen purple juices, standing like ice statues, in a sea of shattered glass. The potatoes froze and rotted in the root cellar. The hibernating bears, miserly squirrels, and forest creatures that found the tall mullein fared better than we did, but not so with the cattle. I heard my parents discussing the losses in low tones and covered my ears with cold hands to shut out the heartbreaking statistics. During the height of one of the worst blizzards, an unscheduled calf was born. It was a beautiful thing, all black with a perfect white heart on its forehead ... Daddy found the mother, half-frozen herself, standing over her baby whose breath the January winds had carried away.

I was weeping as if I would never be able to stop when Gram'ma found me. "Guess what I just heard," she whispered. "Canadian honkers heading back north. And I checked the calendar. Easter's late. That's good: 'Late Easter, early spring.'"

Blindly, I reached for her hand. *"Oh, Gram'ma, Gram'ma, how do you know so much?"*

"It's in the signs," she said comfortingly. "A sort of touchless touching." She reached out and took me in her arms.

I look back on all she taught me — and hope that some day I will be able to pass them on. Memories and love are touchless things. You "just know" when they are there.

For Grandmothers

Grandmothers are all the wonderful things
The mind will never outgrow:
Walks in the woods to find things of spring,
How to cast angels in snow;
Warm chocolate smells when school is let out,
Ears tuned to hear every woe . . .
Grandmothers are all the wonderful things
The mind will never outgrow.

On Being a Surrogate Grandmother

At the turn of the century, sociologists tell us, about half the homes in our country included parents, children, and at least one additional adult relative — usually a grandmother or a grandfather. Now, although more than one-fourth of the American population is made up of people of "grandparent-age," there is no definite ratio of older to younger. In other words, an unknown number of children have never known the warmth and love that grandparents can bring into their lives — just as a growing number of older people have not known the "second spring" of their golden years because they — or their children — have remained childless.

If you are suffering from the "empty arms" syndrome, maybe you would like to consider being a surrogate grandmother. If you *have* thought of it and are wavering, perhaps the following account, used with the permission of Les Hage, will encourage you to make up your mind.

"Come in! Come in!" the cheerful voice greeted anyone who knocked at "Grandma's" door. She didn't ask, "Who?" for everyone was welcome! Such a beautiful, round, smily face, with a number of interesting wrinkles — especially near her eyes, which seemed to say, "I am your friend . . . what can I do for you?"

Mom's dad and mother came from Norway with her, but they had passed away before my recollection of them. Dad's parents stayed in Norway. So I really knew no grandparents at all.

Thus it was that I — along with many of the other children in the neighborhood — came to know Mrs. Borkit as "Grandma." Mother used to send me to buy fresh eggs from her, and on occasion, a stewing hen for Sunday dinner, or cauliflower, eggplant, turnips, or some other vegetables that Dad didn't plant in our garden. Then, each summer she had to take her cow to our pasture with ours and several others in the neighborhood and bring them home at night.

She always had a cookie for me and a cheerful word, "My! you are growing up so fast," which I sorely missed when I left home and returned infrequently for a brief visit.

It was on one such occasion that I learned that "Grandma" was quite ill, so when I knocked at her kitchen door, I wondered if she would hear. That sweet voice, now dimmed with years, sounded from her bedroom, "Come in! Come in!" The friendliness of those words took me back to my boyhood, and the joy I felt when being with "Grandma."

As I sat at her bedside with her hand in mine, we talked about the past. Her husband had died, and my mother had been long gone. Having come to know and accept Jesus as my personal Savior, I wondered if she knew whether my mother was a Christian. She hesitated a while and then told me she wasn't sure. "But you know," she said, "Jesus told us that He would reconcile all things unto Himself in the end," and then reminded me that Paul and Silas told the Philippian jailor, "Believe on the Lord Jesus Christ, and thou shalt be saved — and thy house."

I told her that I always felt there was something very special about her. She explained that her life was changed completely when, as a girl of fourteen, she had accepted Christ as her Savior at a tent meeting in Bavaria.

Many nights since, while awaiting sleep, my thoughts have gone back to "Grandma" and her wonderful revelation that Jesus is in Bavaria, in all the countries and islands of the seas, in my heart, and, hopefully, in all whose lives Christians are privileged to know.

Get involved. Don't let bloodline hinder you from loving!

It Wasn't Very Long Ago...

Do they still harmonize old songs,
The ones we used to sing?
Does honeysuckle cover yet
The old porch and the swing
Where all the couples liked to sit
For moments all alone
Till Little Brother found their spot
And solitude was gone?
Do they still wear those paper hats
And play amusing games?
Now, let's see, whose house was it?
I've forgotten names . . .
I just remember party time
And things we used to do . . .
Molasses cookies, gingerbread . . .
And was there cider, too?
Oh, I remember homemade fudge:
I'd like that recipe . . .
If you have it in some book,
Would you send it to me?
I hope that you remember yet;
It wasn't long ago . . .
How many years, you ask of me?
Oh, just a dream ago.
I'd like to fill my grandkids in
On things that I forget —
They'd like to come and visit
If you still do them yet!

I Recall

I recall a window —
To sit beside and dream —
And a faded Bible
Read in the lamplight gleam.
I recall a rocker
Which took all care away
With its creaking rhythm
At the close of day.
I recall the feathers
Of soft and downy bed,
Where I stole to dreamland
When evening prayers were said.
I recall the comfort
Of drifting off to sleep,
Knowing naught could harm me
In God's and Grandma's keep.

The Daily Things

The daily things I hear and see
Are what make life worthwhile to me:
A mountain standing, etched in gray,
On pink horizons far away . . .
Good-natured brooks beneath the trees . . .
A cooing baby on its knees . . .
A friendly road . . . a book to read . . .
Family love . . . a friend in need . . .
A slanting sun . . . a child-filled tree . . .
Daily things — so dear to me.

So Here We Are at Christmas, Lord

So here we are at Christmas, Lord, with all its breathless expectancy. The air is keen with snow, but our hearts are warmed by the spirit of giving which is rekindled within us. I always hope there will be snow at this season, Lord, because — well, it is so traditional. And I am feeling a special tenderness for the past at this brush-of-the-wings time of year. I remember Christmases gone — the joy, the color, the wonder and magic of it all, made so special by parents and grandparents who wanted me to accept what I would one day give away: this precious set of memories and bright new world of dreams.

And so it is that I thank You, Lord, that I have kept the past as a legacy to share with the young ones underfoot as I drag out the aging ornaments and repeat "The Legend of the Poinsettia" and "The Story of the Christ Child" for the thousandth time. I thank You that they will listen as I talk while scraping celery, stuffing the bird, and unmolding gelatin salads — for, in listening, they will take into their generation a set of memories all their own. In it, may they find courage sufficient for the age in which they live — and hope for the future. I thank You, Lord, for these gifts — greater by far than I can wrap and tie — which my parents and grandparents gave to me.

And thank You, too, Father, for the gifts these children have brought to me! They have recreated in me the joy of playing games, telling stories, and "discovering" a new day. They have given me a new purpose in life, a new importance, a kind of continuity. They *want* to hear my stories over and over, Lord; and they never complain at how slowly I walk or feel embarrassed when I wave good-by until they are out of sight. They like second desserts (as I do!) and enjoy sitting up late at night when there's a special on television! What a luxury they are, Lord. What a blessing! What a gift!

So here we are at Christmas, Lord — back at the manger — and glad to be home!

A Child at Christmas

Someone told you there was no Santa Claus. At first, you were angry with disbelief. Then you were disappointed and hurt, emotions you covered by saying you suspected all along. Then came the sadness, the awful sadness, that you were a child no more. Did it happen that way to you?

When I was a very small child, my parents pulled my sleigh bed (a sort of cradle with curved boards at each end) alongside their heavy four-poster on Christmas Eve. It was a practical arrangement on my mother's part, a device to keep my bare feet from rushing over cold floors to the Christmas tree in the parlor. It was a magical arrangement as far as I was concerned — snuggled between my parents' bed and the cane-bottom, straight-back chair where my black, ribbed stockings hung in waiting. Covered by downy quilts my grandmother had pieced, surrounded by love, and suspended between today and tomorrow, I drifted off to sleep. . . .

Four o'clock! Grandfather's clock and the Rhode Island Red rooster announced the arrival of Christmas Day in perfect synchrony. In the predawn dark that spoke of icicles on the eaves, I would reach out experimentally for the toe of the stuffed stockings. The feel of a wrinkled walnut at the very tip told me, yes, Santa had come! Next, there would be an orange, and after that, untold treasures that my numb fingers tried to guess by squeezing, measuring, and shaking. It was all so wonderfully dreadful — being a child. I cupped my hands and blew on them; I covered my head and curled up like an egg; I shivered deliciously — waiting for the first pink streak of light and the wonderment of discovery. Then I would rip off the bright red and green wrappings in wild abandon . . . all this before the attrition of my belief . . . all this before my new skepticism. . . .

Then the child in me went away, taking with it the sleigh bed and the chair beside it holding stockings which once bulged with mystery. Somebody bought me some bedroom slippers (we called them "house shoes" then) and Grandmother made me a sensible robe. I no longer heard the clock chime four or the rooster make his Christmas morn announcement. I made the annual visit to the decorated tree with my parents. The ribbons were just as shiny, but my heart was no longer light. The presents cost money. They were not gifts from an anonymous donor with a velveteen suit and eight magic reindeer.

As the family grew older we drew names. The practice dwindled to greeting cards as the members went their various ways; and most applauded the greeting-card companies which came up with the idea of printing our names. That saved a lot of time, as did the ready-made fruit cakes that hit the market about the same time. The newspapers made quite an issue of the danger of lighted candles on holiday trees, so we purchased strings of colored lights. But soon we learned that electric bulbs were hazardous, too. Overly-dry needles could catch fire; so we sacrificed the pungent smell of pine for a glistening tinsel tree. The problem with the tinsel tree, of course, was that it was dangerous to use the colored lights, because it conducted electricity. So the tree went away . . . like Santa . . . like the child. . . .

We gave up caroling because everyone was so busy giving parties or going to them that there was nobody left to sing—or sing to. Under social pressure, the school gave up the presentation of the Nativity scene . . . no more Mary and Joseph halting before the inn, and, because there was no room, finding shelter in the stable. They found no shelter at all . . . and they, too, drifted away. . . .

Did it ever occur to you that a Child was the first giver? And that the Christmases you loved so well are not gone, after all? The shortcuts by which society bypassed tradition have turned out to be dead ends. Take note of the "Santa Claus spirit," a legend to be sure, but no longer considered an enemy of childhood. Look at the flood of evergreen trees on the street corners and savor the aroma of the old-fashioned fruit cakes straight out of our grandmothers' cookbooks. People are making gifts by hand as never before; the sale of candles has increased; and the carols are back. Astronomers have rehabilitated the star of Bethlehem and granted that even a King has a birthday!

It is back, the Christmas you knew and loved—in memory and in reality. Your memories may not quite parallel mine, but they are there—the laughing, loving, and giving. For Christmas is the accepting of the greatest gift of all. A too-busy world took a child out of Christmas, but the Child in Christmas came home. And you will guard the precious traditions tenderly ... because *you are a grandmother*!

Please, Lord, a Pair of Green Socks

Pressed to name the single most beautiful thing I've yet to see, I would say, "A pair of green socks." They are my private miracle — still unexplained.

I was spellbound throughout the Christmas concert presented at our church by a visiting junior band. I loved the carols. I admired the "older children" (they were about twelve; I was nine). But I was completely enchanted with a pair of socks one girl wore. They were pine green with fluffy, white angora cuffs — so beautiful they made me ache inside.

"I wish we could afford a pair for you," my mother said wistfully. "They'd be so warm —." My feet were always cold in the harsh winters of my childhood. "But there's simply no way," she said.

I understood. The Great Depression denied us everything short of necessities — even at Christmastime. Our family creed forbade my dropping hints to relatives who might be a wee bit better off. But there *was* a way. . . .

Long ago I had learned not to ask my parents for things I knew they were unable to afford. I knew they were struggling, as were all the other farmers of that time. But I could *pray*. Grandma said that ". . . whatsoever ye shall ask in prayer, believing, ye shall receive" (Matt. 21:22).

So each night I said a long prayer, describing every detail of the coveted socks. I must make God understand exactly the right size and color and why I must depend on Him. Never once did it occur to me that He would fail to hear.

"You see, God, Mama and Daddy don't have the money. The socks would be so warm and I'd take such good care. They ought to be green to match my suit. And the tops have to be white to match the white blouse Mama made for it."

Two days before Christmas a package came from my aunt on my father's side. She lived 200 miles away and would be unable to see us during the holidays, but she sent some souvenirs that had once belonged to my paternal grandmother. Then, at the very bottom of the box, there they were—the answer to my prayers! In my formative theology, God had used my aunt to deliver my miracle, a pair of green socks with fluffy, white cuffs—in exactly the right size.

I am so thankful for a grandmother who taught me that the vital ingredient of prayer is belief that it will be answered. It's the recurring miracle of every Christmas.

Today
I Wrote a Poem

I took her love for granted
As childhood had its way:
There'll always be tomorrow,
Why bother with today?
But things we do in childhood
Aren't easily forgot;
Small things become the great ones,
Though then you think they're not.
She never spoke about it,
But then I guess she knew
A child needs time for growing—
I had my share to do.
Now I remember birthdays
And yule wreaths by the door . . .
Bright-colored eggs at Easter . . .
These memories and more . . .
But more than these, her listening
With tender, silent eyes
To all my then-great troubles,
Then reach for some surprise:
Perhaps a little trinket;
Or just a new-hatched chick—
Arm-in-arm we'd share them
And sharing did the trick.
She tied things up in ribbons
As though life were a toy,
This oh-so-special person
Who filled my life with joy.
Today I wrote a poem:
'Twas just a line or two,
But it will show Grandmother
What memories can do!

A Prayer from
the New Year's Heart

Dear Lord, with hearts still warm from Christmas,
we thank You for yet another gift — Your gift of the New
Year to an old world. How inspiring . . . how comforting

116

. . . like the purity of the new-fallen snow on last year's branches, the new bud on an aging plant, new boots for aging feet, bright fire in a chilly room; and, greatest of all, new hope in an old situation. Lord, we accept Your gifts with humble New Year's hearts.

Last year's hopes and dreams; its fears and tears; its successes and failures; its elevations of joy and deep pits of sorrow belong to yesterday. Ahead lie the clean, white pages of tomorrow, ours to shape with the blessing of time You so generously give us with the turning of the calendar. Oh, Lord, let us use it wisely!

Lord, we know that no one year is complete in Your cycle. Neither does the old year die. You recycle it as the bedding ground, the root, and the seed for another spring, another harvest. And we know that, although the calendar started the rumor, Christmas does not end in a single day. The angels who sang carols of peace and joy are surely singing them still — if we will but listen. The Christmas star shines yet in the galaxy to give us a glimpse of Your glory — if we will but take time to lift our eyes to the brilliant January sky. Remind us, too, Lord, that our giving goes on and on — like Your love — into the repeating decimal of infinity. Let us give throughout this year as You gave — the kind of gifts too large for wrapping, embracing one another as we give with an abundance of love and joy. Let our gifts be a kindly word to the weary stranger, the understanding smile to a tired child . . . forgiveness where there has been doubt . . . and a kind of faith that lights up dark corners with Your love.

Recycle our hearts, Lord, as You recycle our yesterdays. Keep Christmas in our hearts as we meet the needs of family and friends. Remind us this New Year that love is a word that goes on forever!

Grandparents
(To Each Other)

So many things we've shared, my love,
I cannot count them all;
We've built a oneness-kind of house
Where married love grows tall.

We've watched the sun climb up our hill;
We've basked in high-noon rays;
God willing, we'll together view
The sunset of our days.